PRECIOUS MIRROR

Precious Mirror

from the Calligrpahy of

Kobun Chino Otogawa Roshi

with translations by Gary Young

WHITE PINE PRESS | BUFFALO, NEW YORK

ACKNOWLEDGMENTS

Grateful acknowledgment is made to the following magazines where many of these translations previously appeared:

Lumina: "Whatever is"
Miramar: "The truth can be found," "Plum blossoms,"
    "No matter where I look," "Like the full moon"
The Packinghouse Review: "A bird on its long migration,"
    "During the rainy season"
Red Wheelbarrow: "If you want to see," "You can find," "Late at night,"
    "Just thinking of you," "The great promise," "Snow lies in drifts,"
    "The white cloud," "May the moon"
Rowboat: Poetry in Translation: "The winter trees," "An egret"

Printed and bound in the United States of America

First Edition

Cover: Hokyo, *Precious Mirror,* calligraphy by Kobun Chino Otogawa

Library of Congress Control Number: 2017956281

ISBN: 978-1-945680-21-2

White Pine Press
P. O. Box 236
Buffalo, NY 14201

www.whitepine.org

CONTENTS

INTRODUCTION

KOBUN CHINO OTOGAWA was born into the Jokoji
Temple family in Kamo, Niigata Prefecture, Japan in 1938—one
in a long line of Soto Zen priests. Kobun's father died when
Kobun was seven years old, and at the age of thirteen, Kobun was
ordained as a monk by his elder brother, Kin-ei Otogawa Zenji.
Chino is the last name of Kobun's dharma master, Koei Chino
Roshi, who gave him the dharma name of Ho-un, or Phoenix
Cloud. While still a teenager, Kobun studied and practiced zazen
with the preeminent zazen master, Kodo Sawaki Roshi. Kobun
trained at Eiheiji Monastery, and received transmission from his
master there. Kobun then earned a master's degree in Literature
and the Study of Mahayana Buddhism from Kyoto University
under Dr. Keiji Nishitani and Dr. Gadjin Nagao. He returned to
Eiheiji and continued his religious studies for three years, which
when completed enabled him to guide the monastic training of
new monks.

In 1967, Kobun was asked by Suzuki Roshi to come to
California to help establish a monastery at Tassajara in the Carmel
Valley. Suzuki Roshi had also started the San Francisco Zen Center,
where Kobun was actively involved until his death. Kobun also

instituted the monastic practice at Tassajara, where he "welcomed people of any background" to the practice of zazen. Kobun was a singular and extraordinary teacher. His influence was especially felt in California, where he was chief priest at Haiku Zendo in Los Altos, and where he established the Santa Cruz Zen Center, the Spring Mountain Zen Center, Daisho-an in Big Sur, Kannon-do in Mountain View, Jikoji in Los Gatos, Raigo-in in Santa Cruz, and Shingetsu-in at the private summer home of Steve Jobs. Kobun was the subject of a 2012 graphic novel depicting his relationship with Jobs, *The Zen of Steve Jobs*, and his association with Jobs has been depicted in film, books, and even an opera, *The (R)evolution of Steve Jobs*. Kobun also established zendos and temples in Michigan, New Mexico, Austria, and in Switzerland, where Kobun died tragically in 2002 trying to save his young daughter who had fallen into a pond. Both were drowned. At the time of his death, Kobun held the World Wisdom Chair at Naropa University.

Kobun was famously casual, intimate and open. He was comfortable with students addressing him by his first name, and his informality and personal warmth were reflected in his teaching style. His lectures were like poetry, spontaneous and musical. Kobun had a gift for revealing his own intensely personal insights that were rooted in his knowledge of Buddhism, Japanese poetry, Shintoism, Taoism, and Tibetan traditions. Kobun was a master of Zen archery, poetry, and calligraphy. He often stayed up late into the night painting, studying and writing poetry.

Kobun left a vast collection of calligraphy and paintings. Many of his pieces represent original poems, some contain lines from

Zen texts such as *Hokyo Zanmai,* or quotes by Dogen, the monk who brought Soto Zen Buddhism to Japan. Many years ago, I was asked by members of Spring Mountain Zen Center to design and print a fine, letterpress edition of Kobun Otogawa's calligraphy. After spending two years going through hundreds of pieces of Kobun's calligraphy and paintings, I was offered an opportunity to travel to Japan to translate a selection of the work for the book. I was a guest at the Hokyoji Zen Monastery, where I was given access to Dogen's original manuscripts, calligraphy and other relics. I met with Zen priests and Buddhist scholars who were extraordinarily generous with their knowledge of Buddhism, calligraphy, and poetry, and were instrumental to these translations.

I would like to thank Sogyu Fukumura, Keiko Tsuchida, Yasutoshi Yamabuki, Mayumi Yamada, Noriko Hatanaka, Midori Matsuura, Vanja Palmers, and Tanaka Shinkai Roshi, Abbot of Hokyoji, for their support of this project. I am grateful to Asuka and Tomoka Hashimoto, and I would like to give special thanks to Dr. Noritoshi Armaki, Emeritus Professor of Buddhism, Kyoto University, for his generosity and wisdom. Thanks also to Kazuaki Tanahashi, who deciphered sevearl of Kobun's more expressive characters. I would have been unable to complete my translations without their generous help. The biographical information in this introduction was taken primarily from the résumé produced by Kobun in 1992.

This book would not have been possible without the grace and guidance of my dharma companion, Hollis Meyer-deLancey.

Gary Young

for Tanaka Shinkai Roshi

Whatever is—is.
That's really the only law.

If you want to see
the power of the spirit,
it's right in front of you.

The white cloud
reflected in a mirror
cannot speak.

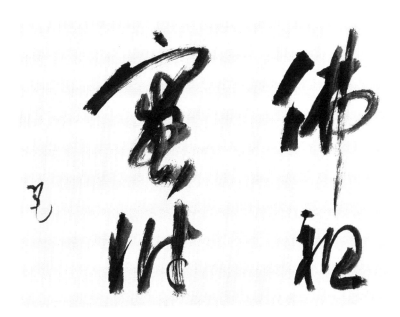

Buddha's intimate secret
has been handed down
from one to another
since the beginning.

一向回來

Wake up
to your original,
unborn self.

I can lead you
to the truth,
but you must
find it for yourself.
Then you'll get the seal.

Look inside
if you want to see
the real light.

The truth can be found
in this world.

君道遠

It's a very long way
to the truth,
but keep going, dear friend,
you'll get there.

Thunder Phoenix

Snow Phoenix

Spirit Phoenix

I connect
to the spirit.

The only time you have
is now.

梅

月

雪

Plum blossoms
lit by moonlight
are the color of snow.

佛法

僧寶

We become jewels
when we come to the truth.

少欲者有坦然之乐
多欲者有烦恼之苦

You can find
perfect peace
if you desire nothing.

The winter trees
are in flower
with blossoms of snow.

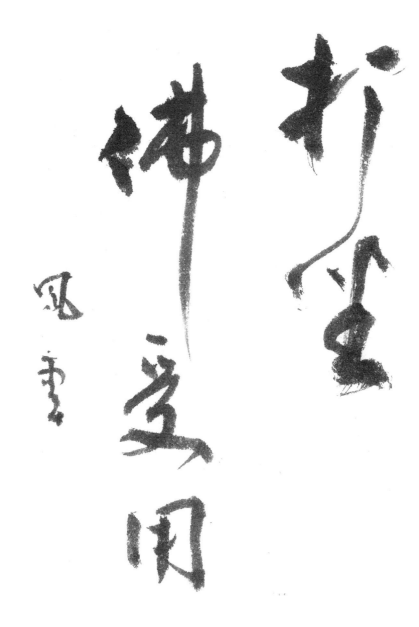

Just sit—
you're pleasing
the Buddha.

現身

風書

The Buddha
is present
in this very body.

如龍得水

混書

Be like the dragon,
and go where you must
to find water.

佛祖

子孫

The Buddha is here
in my daughter,
the dragon girl.

その庭に
羽を休めし
渡り鳥

名もしらぬまた
飛び起ちにけり

昌

A bird on its long migration
stopped to rest in my garden,
but flew away
before I could learn his name.

The great promise
hidden within you
is boundless.

A silver bowl
has been filled with snow.

An egret
flies across the full moon
and disappears.

隱聲高
平月雨
虹橋淡
連峯間

乃廿八字遠歌、

寫

During the rainy season,
the little stream became
a roaring torrent,
and a rainbow appeared
like a bridge across the mountains.

桑王访
女夜梦
昂龙桥
无声曲

乡村八月免歌二

The Medicine Buddha
rested here last night
in a dream.

I saw a waterfall
and a flying dragon,
but no sun.

清川

珠

雪

川

昆

Snow lies in drifts
beneath a clear, full moon.

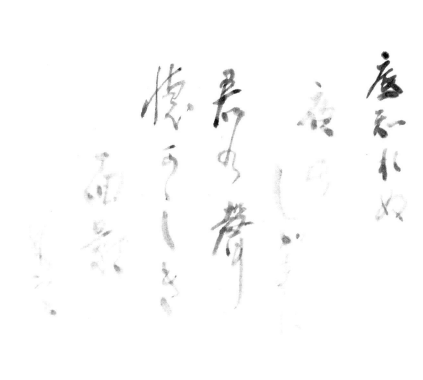

庭をれぬ
夜もしぐれ
君の聲
恨うしさ
雨氣

Late at night
I remember your face,
and in the dark,
I think I hear your voice.

こころ
ゆくもる

Just thinking of you
has warmed my heart.

Like the full moon,
a pure heart shines.

光涛

見证艺术

May the moon
bathe us
in its pure, cool light.

You are a bell
made of jade.

Up early,
you step
 on pearls of dew.

Be exactly
who you are.

No matter where I look,
it's beautiful.

When you shoot
an arrow at yourself,
make sure your aim is true.

Sitting
is an open gate
to a land
of perfect peace.

Don't be afraid
to wake up
your spirit.

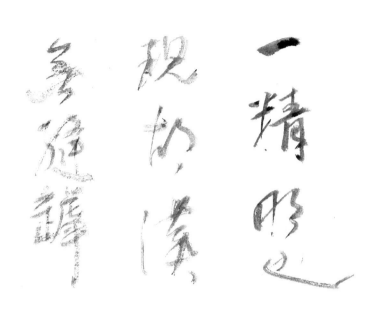

一精明，

税切深，

多施镇

Don't jump to conclusions;
that lively old man
may look like a stranger,
but you never know
who he might be.

NOTES

13   The first line of *Hokyo Zanmai.*

15   Kobun is using his own calligraphy as an example of 'jin tsu riki', spiritual or supernatural power.

17   Kobun makes reference to the title of *Hokyo Zanmai,* 'Precious Mirror', and also offers a visual pun by writing the character for 'cloud' in mirror writing.

19   The second line of *Hokyo Zanmai.*

23   It is important for a Zen master to give proof—his seal—that his dharma has been passed on to a disciple.

27   Another take on the first line of *Hokyo Zanmai.*

31   Kobun's dharma name was Ho Un—Phoenix Cloud. This and the following two, nearly identical pieces, were executed as a group, and were probably written in New Mexico during a storm.

39   A quote from Dogen, the first Patriarch of Soto Zen Buddhism.

49   From a remark by Dogen.

51   A phrase from Dogen.

53   The dragon represents water, and its transformative powers.

55   Kobun conflates his own daughter with the Dragon King's daughter, who achieves instant enlightenment in the Lotus Sutra.

57   Birds often stopped at Kobun's childhood home on their migration south from Siberia.

61   This page and the next are successive lines from *Hokyo Zanmai.*

67   The Medicine Buddha (also referred to as the Healing Buddha or Medicine King) appeared to Kobun in a dream while at Tassajara.

77	The moon is a symbol of Buddhist truths, and represents the earthly truth of Buddhism.
79	A dharma name.
83	An expression of Buddhism as ultimate affirmation.
87	To penetrate oneself with an arrow is to open oneself to the truths of Buddhism.
89	A phrase from Dogen. By sitting, he of course means sitting zazen.
93	The appearance of a foreigner in Buddhist poems is generally meant to suggest Bodhidharma, the man who brought Zen Buddhism to China.

photo © by Nicolas Schossleitner

BIOGRAPHIES

Kobun Chino Otogawa Roshi was born in Kamo, Niigata Prefecture, Japan in 1938. He was from a long line of Soto Zen priests. In 1967 he was asked by Suzuki Roshi, the Zen priest who started the Zen Center in San Francisco, to come to California to help establish Tassajara. Kobun taught there, and in various other temples for many years. He also held the the World Wisdom Chair at Naropa University. Kobun was a skilled calligrapher, painter, and was a master of Zen archery. He died tragically in 2002 trying to save his young daughter who had fallen into a pond; they both drowned. Kobun's fame outside of the Zen community rests with his connection to Steve Jobs. Kobun taught Jobs Zen, lived in his house for a time, and married Jobs and his wife. Kobun is the subject of a graphic novel depicting his relationship with Jobs, *The Zen of Steve Jobs.*

Gary Young is a poet and artist whose books include *Hands, The Dream of A Moral Life, Days, Braver Deeds, Pleasure,* and *Even So: New and Selected Poems*, published by White Pine Press. His book *No Other Life* won the William Carlos Williams Award, and in 2009 he received the Shelley Memorial Award from the Poetry Society of America. His latest book, *That's What I Thought,* won the Lexi Rudnitzky Editor's Choice Award from Persea Books. He teaches Creative Writing and directs the Cowell Press at UC Santa Cruz.

Companions for the Journey Series

Inspirational work by well-known writers in a small-book format
designed to be carried along on your journey through life.

Volume 18
Breaking the Willow
Poems of Parting, Exile, Separation and Return
Translated by David Lunde
978-1-893996-95-3   96 pages

Volume 17
The Secret Gardens of Mogador
A Novel by Alberto Ruy-Sanchez
Translated by Rhonda Dahl Buchanan
978-1-893996-99-1   240 pages

Volume 16
Majestic Nights
Love Poems of Bengali Women
Translated by Carolyne Wright and co-translators
978-1-893996-93-9   108 pages

Volume 15
Dropping the Bow
Poems from Ancient India
Translated by Andrew Schelling
978-1-893996-96-0   128 pages

Volume 6
A Zen Forest: Zen Sayings
Translated by Soioku Shigematsu
Preface by Gary Snyder
1-893996-30-1   120 pages

Volume 5
Back Roads to Far Towns: Basho's Travel Journal
Translated by Cid Corman
1-893996-31-X   94 pages

Volume 4
Heaven My Blanket, Earth My Pillow
Poems from Sung Dynasty China by Yang Wan-Li
Translated by Jonathan Chaves
1-893996-29-8   288 pages

Volume 3
10,000 Dawns: The Love Poems of Claire and Yvan Goll
Translated by Thomas Rain Crowe and Nan Watkins
1-893996-27-1   88 pages

Volume 2
There Is No Road: Proverbs by Antonio Machado
Translated by Mary G. Berg and Dennis Maloney
1-893996-66-2   118 pages

Volume I
Wild Ways: Zen Poems of Ikkyu
Translated by John Stevens
1-893996-65-4   152 pages